The Physicists

Works by Friedrich Dürrenmatt
available from Grove Press

The Physicists
The Visit

FRIEDRICH DÜRRENMATT

The Physicists
A Comedy in Two Acts

Translated from the German by Joel Agee

Grove Press
New York

Originally published in Switzerland under the title *Die Physiker* (*The Physicists*), published by Verlag der Arche, Zürich 1962 and revised version by Diogenes Verlag AG, Zürich 1980. Joel Agee translation originally published in *Selected Writings, Volume 1: Plays,* 2006, by The University Chicago Press, Chicago.

Printed in the United States of America

ISBN: 978-0-8021-4427-0

Grove Press
an imprint of Grove/Atlantic, Inc.
841 Broadway
New York, NY 10003

Distributed by Publishers Group West

www.groveatlantic.com

17 18 19 20   9 8 7 6 5 4 3 2

For Therese Giehse

Characters

FRÄULEIN DOCTOR MATHILDE VON ZAHND	*Psychiatrist*
MARTA BOLL	*Head nurse*
MONIKA STETTLER	*Nurse*
UWE SIEVERS	*Chief male nurse*
McARTHUR	*Male nurse*
MURILLO	*Male nurse*
HERBERT GEORG BEUTLER, AKA "NEWTON"	*Patient*
ERNST HEINRICH ERNESTI, AKA "EINSTEIN"	*Patient*
JOHANN WILHELM MÖBIUS	*Patient*
OSKAR ROSE	*A missionary*
LINA ROSE	*His wife*
ADOLF-FRIEDRICH	
WILFRIED-KASPAR	*Their sons*
JÖRG-LUKAS	
RICHARD VOSS	*Police inspector*
GUHL	*Policeman*
BLOCHER	*Policeman*
	Forensic doctor

The Physicists

ACT ONE

*Place: The drawing room of a comfortable though somewhat run-down
villa belonging to Les Cerisiers, a private sanatorium.*

*Immediate neighborhood: A lakeside, in its natural state at first,
then cluttered with buildings, and later a medium-sized, almost small
town.*

*The once attractive little place with its castle and old town is now graced
by hideous buildings housing insurance companies and is mainly supported
by a modest university with an extensive department of theology and
summer courses in foreign languages; further by a business college and a
school of dentistry; a boarding school for girls; and finally by various light
industries that are hardly worth mentioning. These features alone indicate
a remove from the hub of commerce. A rather superfluous addition is the
calming influence supplied by the landscape: blue mountain ranges, hills
covered with trees on a scale that does not dwarf humanity, a sizable lake,
and nearby, a wide plain that turns misty in the evening, once a dismal
swamp but now traversed by irrigation trenches and therefore quite fertile.
There is a prison somewhere, complete with a large agricultural plant. As a
result, silent and shadowy groups and scatterings of hoeing and digging
criminals can be seen everywhere. However, the location plays no part in
our play and we mention it only for the sake of precision. For we never
leave the villa of the insane asylum (there, the word slipped out after all).
Or, to be more exact: we won't even leave the drawing room, for we have
decided to adhere strictly to the unities of place, time, and action. An
action that takes place among madmen requires classical form.*

*But let's get down to business. The villa was where all the patients
of the establishment's founder, Fräulein Dr. h.c. Dr. med.* Mathilda*

---

*The accretion of titles indicates that their bearer is unmarried (Fräulein), that
she has received an honorary doctorate (h.c., standing for "honoris causa"),
and that she is a medical doctor.

von Zahnd, used to be housed: rundown aristocrats, arteriosclerotic politicians (unless still in office), debilitated millionaires, schizophrenic writers, manic-depressive industrialists, and so on, in short, the entire mentally disturbed elite of half the Western world. For the Fräulein Doctor is famous, not only because the hunchbacked spinster in her eternal white smock is the last noteworthy descendant of a family that once held great power in the region, but also because she is a humanitarian and psychiatrist of note, indeed, we can safely say, of international distinction (her correspondence with C. G. Jung has just been published). But now the prominent and not always pleasant patients have long since moved into the elegant, well-lit new building, where for horrendous fees even the most vicious past is turned into pure enjoyment. The new building spreads over the southern section of the extensive park, branching out into various pavilions (with stained-glass windows by Erni in the chapel) in the direction of the plain, while the villa's lawn, equipped with gigantic trees, descends toward the lake. There is a stone embankment along the edge of the lake.

The drawing room of the now sparsely occupied villa is mostly frequented by three patients, who happen to be physicists. Actually this is not entirely a matter of chance, for humane principles are applied here, and birds of a feather are encouraged to flock together. The three men live for themselves, each one wrapped in the cocoon of his imaginary world, taking their meals together in the drawing room, occasionally discussing some scientific matter or else quietly staring into space—harmless, lovable lunatics, amenable, easy to treat, and quite undemanding. In a word, they would be model patients, were it not for certain grave, indeed horrible, recent events: three months ago, one of them strangled a nurse, and now the same thing has happened again. Consequently, the police are back in the house. The drawing room, therefore, is more populated than usual. The nurse is lying on the parquet floor, in a tragic and definitive position, somewhat in the background, so as not to alarm the audience unnecessarily. But it is impossible not to see that a struggle has taken place. The furniture is in considerable disarray. A floor lamp and two chairs are lying on the floor, and downstage left a round table has tipped over in such a way that its legs jut out at the audience.

Apart from all this, the villa's transformation into an insane asylum (it used to be the von Zahnds' summer residence) has left painful traces in the drawing room. The walls have been covered to a height of six feet with hygienic glossy paint; the original plaster emerges above that, with partially preserved stucco moldings. The three doors in the background, leading from a small hall into the physicists' rooms, are padded with black leather. In addition, they are numbered one to three. To the left of the hall is an ugly central-heating unit; to the right, a washbasin with towels on a rail.

The sound of a violin, accompanied by piano, comes from room number two (the middle room). Beethoven. Kreutzer Sonata. To the left is the wall overlooking the park, with high windows that reach down to the parquet floor, which is covered with linoleum. Heavy curtains hang to the left and right of the windows. The glass doors lead on to a terrace, whose stone balustrade stands out against the green of the park and the relatively sunny November weather. It is shortly after 4:30 p.m. To the right, over an unused fireplace with a fire screen in front of it, hangs a portrait, in a heavy gold frame, of an old man with a pointed beard. Downstage right, a heavy oak door. A heavy chandelier is suspended from the brown, coffered ceiling. The furniture: next to the round table—that is, when the room is in order—there are three chairs. Like the table, they are painted white. The remaining furniture, with somewhat worn upholstery, belongs to various periods. Downstage right, a sofa with a small table flanked by two armchairs. The floor lamp actually belongs behind the sofa, so the room is not cluttered at all. Not much is required for the sets of a stage on which, contrary to the plays of the ancients, the satire precedes the tragedy. We can begin.

Policemen in plain clothes are busying themselves with the corpse—imperturbable, good-natured fellows who have already consumed their portion of white wine and whose breath smells accordingly. They take measurements, take the dead nurse's fingerprints, draw a chalk contour *of her body on the floor, and so on. In the middle of the room stands Police Inspector Richard Voss, wearing a coat and a hat; on the left is the* HEAD NURSE, *Marta Boll, looking intensely resolute. In the armchair on the far right sits a policeman, taking notes in shorthand. The* INSPECTOR *takes a cigar out of a brown cigar case.*

INSPECTOR Smoking's allowed, isn't it?

HEAD NURSE It's not customary.

INSPECTOR Sorry. (*He puts the cigar back.*)

HEAD NURSE A cup of tea?

INSPECTOR I'd prefer schnapps.

HEAD NURSE This is a sanatorium.

INSPECTOR Then nothing. Blocher, you can take pictures.

BLOCHER Yes, sir.

Photographs are taken. Flashes.

INSPECTOR What was the nurse's name?

HEAD NURSE Irene Straub.

INSPECTOR Age?

HEAD NURSE Twenty-two. From Kohlwang.

INSPECTOR Family?

HEAD NURSE A brother in eastern Switzerland.

INSPECTOR Notified?

HEAD NURSE By telephone.

INSPECTOR The murderer?

HEAD NURSE Please, Inspector—the poor man is ill.

INSPECTOR   All right: the perpetrator?

HEAD NURSE   Ernst Heinrich Ernesti. We call him Einstein.

INSPECTOR   Why?

HEAD NURSE   Because he thinks he's Einstein.

INSPECTOR   I see. (*He turns to the Policeman, who is taking notes.*)   Do you have the head nurse's statements, Guhl?

GUHL   Yes, sir.

INSPECTOR   Also strangled, doctor?

FORENSIC DOCTOR   Definitely. With the cord of the floor lamp. These madmen often develop tremendous strength. There's something grand about it.

INSPECTOR   Hm. You think so? In that case I find it irresponsible to leave these madmen in the care of female nurses. This is already the second murder—

HEAD NURSE   Please, Inspector.

INSPECTOR   —the second accident within three months in the asylum known as Les Cerisiers. (*He pulls out a notebook.*) On August twelve, a certain Herbert Georg Beutler, who considers himself to be the great physicist Newton, strangled the nurse Dorothea Moser. (*He puts the notebook back.*) Also in this room. This would not have happened with male attendants.

HEAD NURSE   You think so? Dorothea Moser was a member of the League of Lady Wrestlers and Nurse Straub was regional champion of the National Judo Association.

INSPECTOR   And you?

HEAD NURSE   I lift weights.

5

INSPECTOR   May I now see the murderer?

HEAD NURSE   Please, Inspector.

INSPECTOR   I mean the perpetrator.

HEAD NURSE   He's fiddling.

INSPECTOR   What do you mean, fiddling?

HEAD NURSE   You can hear it.

INSPECTOR   Then tell him to stop. (*Since the Head Nurse does not react:*)   I need to ask him some questions.

HEAD NURSE   Can't be done.

INSPECTOR   Why not?

HEAD NURSE   We can't allow that, for medical reasons. Mr. Ernesti has to play his fiddle now.

INSPECTOR   But this fellow strangled a nurse!

HEAD NURSE   Inspector, this is not a fellow, but a sick human being who needs to calm down. And since he thinks he is Einstein, he only calms down when he's playing his violin.

INSPECTOR   Am I losing my mind?

HEAD NURSE   No.

INSPECTOR   I'm getting confused. (*He wipes the sweat from his brow.*)   It's hot in here.

HEAD NURSE   Not at all.

INSPECTOR   Nurse, please ask the chief psychiatrist to come here.

HEAD NURSE   That's not possible either. Doctor von Zahnd is accompanying Einstein on the piano. Einstein only calms down when the doctor does the accompaniment.

6

INSPECTOR   And three months ago Doctor von Zahnd had to play chess with Newton so that he could calm down. I'm not buying that any longer, Miss Boll. I simply have to speak to the head psychiatrist.

HEAD NURSE   All right. Then you have to wait.

INSPECTOR   How long will this fiddling go on?

HEAD NURSE   A quarter of an hour, an hour. It depends.

INSPECTOR (*controlling himself*)   Fine. I'm waiting. (*He roars:*) I'm waiting!

BLOCHER   We're just about finished, Inspector.

INSPECTOR (*gloomily*)   So am I.

Silence. The Inspector wipes sweat from his brow.

INSPECTOR (*cont.*)   You can remove the body.

BLOCHER   Yes, sir.

HEAD NURSE   I'll show the gentlemen the way through the park to the chapel.

She opens the french windows. The body is carried out. The equipment likewise. The Inspector takes off his hat, sits down, exhausted, in the armchair to the left of the sofa. Violin with piano accompaniment continues. Then out of room number three comes Herbert Georg Beutler in early eighteenth-century costume with wig.

NEWTON   Sir Isaac Newton.

INSPECTOR   Police Inspector Richard Voss. (*He remains seated.*)

NEWTON   Pleased to meet you. Very pleased. Really. I heard pounding noises, groaning, gasping, then people coming and going. May I ask what's going on?

7

INSPECTOR Nurse Irene Straub has been strangled.

NEWTON The regional champion of the National Judo Association?

INSPECTOR The regional champion.

NEWTON Terrible.

INSPECTOR By Ernst Heinrich Ernesti.

NEWTON But he's playing the violin.

INSPECTOR He has to calm down.

NEWTON The struggle must have taken a lot out of him. He's rather frail. What did he use to—

INSPECTOR The cord of the floor lamp.

NEWTON The cord of the floor lamp. That's one way to do it. Ernesti. I'm sorry for him. Extremely sorry. And I'm sorry for the judo champion too. Excuse me, please. I have to do some straightening up.

INSPECTOR Be my guest. Our work is done.

Newton sets the table upright and then the chairs.

NEWTON I can't stand disorder. Actually, I became a physicist only because of my love of order. (*He rights the floor lamp.*) To prove that the apparent disorder of nature is founded in a higher order. (*He lights a cigarette.*) Do you mind if I smoke?

INSPECTOR (*pleased*) On the contrary, I—(*He is about to take a cigar from his case.*)

NEWTON Excuse me, but since we were just talking about order: only patients are allowed to smoke here, not visitors. Otherwise the room would be impossible to breathe in.

INSPECTOR I understand. (*He puts the cigar case back in his pocket.*)

NEWTON Do you mind if I have a little glass of cognac?

INSPECTOR Not at all.

Newton takes a bottle of cognac and a glass from behind the fire screen.

NEWTON Ernesti—I can't believe it. I'm really upset. How could anyone strangle a nurse? (*He sits down on the sofa, pours himself cognac.*)

INSPECTOR But you yourself have strangled a nurse.

NEWTON Me?

INSPECTOR Dorothea Moser.

NEWTON The wrestler?

INSPECTOR On August twelfth. With the curtain cord.

NEWTON But that's a completely different matter, Inspector. After all, I'm not crazy. To your health.

INSPECTOR To yours.

Newton drinks.

NEWTON Dorothea Moser. When I think back: straw-blonde hair. Remarkably strong. Supple despite her bulk. She loved me, and I loved her. A dilemma that could only by resolved by means of a curtain cord.

INSPECTOR Dilemma?

NEWTON My mission is to think about gravity, not to love a woman.

INSPECTOR I understand.

NEWTON   And besides, there was the enormous difference in age.

INSPECTOR   That's true. You must be well over two hundred years old.

NEWTON (*stares at him uncomprehendingly*)   How do you mean?

INSPECTOR   Well, as Newton—

NEWTON   Are you a little bit touched, Inspector, or are you just pretending?

INSPECTOR   Now look—

NEWTON   Do you really believe that I'm Newton?

INSPECTOR   Well, you believe it.

Newton looks around suspiciously.

NEWTON   May I tell you a secret, Inspector? In confidence?

INSPECTOR   Of course.

NEWTON   I am not Sir Isaac. I just pretend to be Newton.

INSPECTOR   And why?

NEWTON   So as not to confuse Ernesti.

INSPECTOR   I don't get it.

NEWTON   Unlike me, Ernesti is really sick. He thinks he's Albert Einstein.

INSPECTOR   What does that have to do with you?

NEWTON   If Ernesti found out that I'm actually Albert Einstein, all hell would break loose.

INSPECTOR   Are you saying—?

NEWTON Yes. The famous physicist, discoverer of the theory of relativity, that's me. Born March fourteenth, eighteen seventy-nine, in the city of Ulm.

The Inspector stands, somewhat bewildered.

INSPECTOR Pleased to meet you.

Newton also rises.

NEWTON Just call me Albert.

INSPECTOR You can call me Richard.

They shake hands.

NEWTON I can assure you that I would fiddle my way through the Kreutzer Sonata with a good deal more brio than Ernst Heinrich Ernesti just did. The way he plays the andante is simply barbaric, don't you think?

INSPECTOR I don't know anything about music.

NEWTON Why don't we sit?

He pulls the Inspector down onto the sofa and puts an arm around his shoulder.

NEWTON (*cont.*) Richard.

INSPECTOR Albert?

NEWTON It bothers you, doesn't it, Richard, that you can't arrest me?

INSPECTOR But Albert.

NEWTON Would you like to arrest me because I strangled the nurse or because I made the atomic bomb possible?

INSPECTOR But Albert.

NEWTON When you turn that knob next to the door, what happens, Richard?

INSPECTOR The light goes on.

NEWTON You establish an electric contact. Do you know anything about electricity, Richard?

INSPECTOR I'm not a physicist.

NEWTON I don't know much about it either. All I do is set up a theory based on observations of nature. I write down this theory in the language of mathematics and arrive at several formulas. That's where the engineers come in. All they're concerned with are the formulas. They treat electricity the way a pimp treats a whore. They exploit it. They build machines, and a machine doesn't work until it becomes independent of the knowledge that led to its invention. So any fool nowadays can switch on a light—or detonate an atomic bomb. (*He pats the Inspector on the shoulder.*) And now you want to arrest me for that, Richard. That's not fair.

INSPECTOR I don't want to arrest you at all, Albert.

NEWTON Only because you think I'm insane. But why don't you refuse to switch on a light if you don't understand anything about electricity? You are the criminal here, Richard. But now I must put my cognac away, otherwise the head nurse will throw a fit. (*Newton hides the cognac bottle behind the fire screen but leaves the glass standing.*) Good-bye.

INSPECTOR Good-bye, Albert.

NEWTON You should arrest yourself, Richard! (*He disappears into room number three.*)

INSPECTOR Now I'm just going to smoke.

With a decisive air, he takes a cigar from his cigar case and smokes.
Blocher comes in through the french doors.

BLOCHER We're ready to leave, Inspector.

The Inspector stamps his foot.

INSPECTOR I'm waiting! For the head psychiatrist!

BLOCHER Yes, sir.

The Inspector calms down, grumbling.

INSPECTOR Drive back to town with the men, Blocher; I'll
leave later.

BLOCHER All right, sir.

Exit Blocher.

*The Inspector puffs his cigar, stands up, stomps around the drawing room
with a defiant air, stops to gaze at the portrait above the fireplace. Mean-
while the violin and piano have stopped. The door to room number two
opens and Fräulein DOCTOR MATHILDE VON ZAHND
comes out. Hunchbacked, about fifty-five, white smock, stethoscope.*

DOCTOR VON ZAHND My father, Privy Councillor August
von Zahnd. He used to live in this villa before I turned it
into a sanatorium. A great man, a true human being. I am
his only child. He hated me like the plague. Actually he
hated everyone like the plague. Probably with good reason.
As a major industrialist he saw depths of depravity that are
forever hidden from our profession. We psychiatrists are still
hopelessly romantic philanthropists.

INSPECTOR Three months ago there was a different portrait
hanging here.

DOCTOR VON ZAHND My uncle, the politician. Chancellor
Joachim von Zahnd. (*She puts the music score on the small table*

in front of the sofa.) All right. Ernesti has calmed down. He threw himself onto his bed and went to sleep. Like a happy little boy. I can breathe freely again. I was afraid he'd want to play Brahms's Third Sonata as well. (*She sits down on the armchair to the left of the sofa.*)

INSPECTOR Excuse me, Doctor von Zahnd, for transgressing the no-smoking rule, but—

DOCTOR VON ZAHND Enjoy your cigar, Inspector. The head nurse may not like it, but I need a cigarette myself. Rather urgently. Give me a light.

He gives her a light, she smokes.

DOCTOR VON ZAHND (*cont.*) Awful. Poor Irene. Such a clean young thing. (*She notices the glass.*) Newton?

INSPECTOR I had the pleasure.

DOCTOR VON ZAHND I'd better put the glass away.

Before she can take the glass, he does and puts it behind the fire screen.

DOCTOR VON ZAHND (*cont.*) On account of the head nurse.

INSPECTOR I understand.

DOCTOR VON ZAHND You had a conversation with Newton?

INSPECTOR I discovered something. (*He sits down on the sofa.*)

DOCTOR VON ZAHND Congratulations.

INSPECTOR In reality, Newton thinks he's Einstein as well.

DOCTOR VON ZAHND That's what he tells everybody. But actually he believes he's Newton.

INSPECTOR (*taken aback*) Are you sure?

DOCTOR VON ZAHND It's I who decides who my patients think they are. I know them far better than they know themselves.

INSPECTOR Could be. But in that case you should help us, Doctor. The government is complaining.

DOCTOR VON ZAHND The district attorney?

INSPECTOR Furious.

DOCTOR VON ZAHND As if that were my concern, Voss.

INSPECTOR Two murders—

DOCTOR VON ZAHND Please, Inspector.

INSPECTOR Two accidents. In three months. You have to admit that security measures in your establishment leave something to be desired.

DOCTOR VON ZAHND What sort of security measures are you imagining, Inspector? I'm running a sanatorium, not a penal institution. Even in your line of work, Inspector, you can't lock murderers up before they've committed their murders.

INSPECTOR Except in this case, we're not dealing with murderers but with madmen, and they can kill at any time.

DOCTOR VON ZAHND So do normal people, and much more frequently. I have only to think of my grandfather Leonidas von Zahnd, the field marshal, with his great, lost war. What age are we living in? Has medical science made progress or not? Don't we have new resources at our disposal, drugs that can transform raving madmen into gentle lambs? Are we supposed to lock up the mentally ill again, put them in solitary, or suspend them in nets, wearing boxing gloves, the way it used to be done? As if we were unable to tell the difference between dangerous and harmless patients.

INSPECTOR   Evidently you failed to make this distinction in the cases of Beutler and Ernesti.

DOCTOR VON ZAHND   Unfortunately. This is what troubles me, not your enraged district attorney.

EINSTEIN *comes out of room number two, carrying his violin. Lean, with long, snow-white hair and mustache.*

EINSTEIN   I woke up.

DOCTOR VON ZAHND   Come now, Professor.

EINSTEIN   Did I play well?

DOCTOR VON ZAHND   Beautifully, Professor.

EINSTEIN   What about Irene? Is she—?

DOCTOR VON ZAHND   Don't give it another thought, Professor.

EINSTEIN   I'm going back to sleep.

DOCTOR VON ZAHND   That's good of you, Professor.

Einstein goes back into his room. The Inspector has leapt to his feet.

INSPECTOR   So that was him!

DOCTOR VON ZAHND   Ernst Heinrich Ernesti.

INSPECTOR   The murderer—

DOCTOR VON ZAHND   Please, Inspector.

INSPECTOR   The perpetrator, the one who thinks he's Einstein. When was he committed?

DOCTOR VON ZAHND   Two years ago.

INSPECTOR   And Newton?

DOCTOR VON ZAHND   One year ago. They're both incurable. God knows, Voss, I'm no beginner in my profession, you know this and so does the district attorney. He has always respected my psychiatric reports. My sanatorium is world famous and correspondingly expensive. I can't afford to make mistakes, and I certainly can't afford incidents that bring the police into my house. If anyone is to blame here, it is medical science, not I. These unfortunate accidents could not have been foreseen. You or I would be just as likely to strangle a nurse. Medically, there is no explanation for what has happened. Unless—

She has taken a new cigarette. The Inspector lights it for her.

DOCTOR VON ZAHND (*cont.*)   Inspector. Haven't you noticed something?

INSPECTOR   Such as?

DOCTOR VON ZAHND   Consider the two patients.

INSPECTOR   Yes?

DOCTOR VON ZAHND   They are both physicists. Nuclear physicists.

INSPECTOR   So?

DOCTOR VON ZAHND   You really have an unsuspecting mind, Inspector.

INSPECTOR (*pondering*)   Doctor.

DOCTOR VON ZAHND   Voss?

INSPECTOR   You think—?

DOCTOR VON ZAHND They were both experimenting with radioactive materials.

INSPECTOR You suspect a connection?

DOCTOR VON ZAHND I am merely stating the facts, that's all. Both of them go insane, the condition of both deteriorates, both become a threat to the community, both of them strangle nurses.

INSPECTOR You think their brains could have been affected by—radioactivity?

DOCTOR VON ZAHND Unfortunately, this is a possibility I must face.

INSPECTOR (*looking around*) What's behind this door?

DOCTOR VON ZAHND The hall, the green drawing room, and the second floor.

INSPECTOR How many patients are still here?

DOCTOR VON ZAHND Three.

INSPECTOR Only?

DOCTOR VON ZAHND The rest were moved to the new house immediately after the first accident. Fortunately I was able to complete the building just in time. Rich patients and also my relatives contributed to the costs. By dying. Most of them here. I became the sole heir. Destiny, Voss. I am always the sole heir. My family is so old that it's almost a small medical miracle that I can pass for relatively normal, mentally, that is.

INSPECTOR (*thinking*) The third patient?

DOCTOR VON ZAHND Also a physicist.

INSPECTOR   Strange. Don't you think?

DOCTOR VON ZAHND   I don't think so at all. I sort my patients. Writers with writers, industrialists with industrialists, millionairesses with millionairesses, and physicists with physicists.

INSPECTOR   His name?

DOCTOR VON ZAHND   Johann Wilhelm Möbius.

INSPECTOR   Was he involved with radioactivity as well?

DOCTOR VON ZAHND   No.

INSPECTOR   Could he also—

DOCTOR VON ZAHND   He's been here for fifteen years, harmless, and his condition has never changed.

INSPECTOR   Doctor von Zahnd. You can't get around it. The district attorney categorically insists on male attendants for your physicists.

DOCTOR VON ZAHND   He shall have them.

INSPECTOR (*reaching for his hat*)   Good. I'm glad you agree. I have now paid two visits to Les Cerisiers, Doctor von Zahnd. I hope I won't have to show up here again.

He puts on his hat, goes out left through the french doors on to the terrace, and walks away through the park. Fräulein Doctor Mathilde von Zahnd looks after him thoughtfully. Head Nurse Marta Boll enters right, stops short, sniffing the air. She is holding a file folder.

HEAD NURSE   Please, Doctor—

DOCTOR VON ZAHND   Oh, excuse me. (*She extinguishes the cigarette.*)   Have they laid out Irene Straub?

HEAD NURSE   Under the organ.

DOCTOR VON ZAHND Have them put candles around her, and wreaths.

HEAD NURSE I've already called the florist about it.

DOCTOR VON ZAHND How is my aunt Senta?

HEAD NURSE Restless.

DOCTOR VON ZAHND Double her dose. And my cousin Ulrich?

HEAD NURSE Closed ward.

DOCTOR VON ZAHND Miss Boll, I must unfortunately put an end to one of our traditions at Les Cerisiers. Until now I have employed female nurses only. As of tomorrow, the villa will be supervised by male nurses.

HEAD NURSE Doctor von Zahnd, I will not permit anyone to deprive me of my three physicists. They are my most interesting cases.

DOCTOR VON ZAHND My decision is final.

HEAD NURSE I'd like to know where you'll find the male nurses. Given the high demand for them these days.

DOCTOR VON ZAHND Let me worry about that. Has Mrs. Möbius arrived?

HEAD NURSE She's waiting in the green room.

DOCTOR VON ZAHND Send her in.

HEAD NURSE Möbius's medical history.

DOCTOR VON ZAHND Thank you.

The Head Nurse hands her the file, then goes out the door on the right, but turns before leaving.

HEAD NURSE But—

DOCTOR VON ZAHND Please, Nurse, please.

Exit Head Nurse. Doctor von Zahnd opens the file, studies it at the round table. The Head Nurse enters, leading MRS. ROSE and three boys, fourteen, fifteen, and sixteen years old. The eldest is carrying a briefcase. MR. ROSE, a missionary, brings up the rear. Doctor von Zahnd rises.

DOCTOR VON ZAHND Dear Mrs. Möbius—

MRS. ROSE Rose. Mrs. Rose. This will be a cruel surprise for you, Doctor: three weeks ago I married Mr. Rose, a missionary. A little suddenly, perhaps. We met in September at a convention. (*She blushes and somewhat awkwardly indicates her new husband.*) Oskar was a widower.

DOCTOR VON ZAHND (*shaking her hand.*) Congratulations, Mrs. Rose. From the bottom of my heart. To you, too, Mr. Rose. Best wishes. (*She nods in his direction.*)

MRS. ROSE You do understand why we took this step?

DOCTOR VON ZAHND But of course, Mrs. Rose. Life must continue to flower.

MR. ROSE How quiet it is here! How friendly. A truly divine peace reigns in this house, quite as the psalmist says: for the Lord heareth the needy and despiseth not his prisoners.

MRS. ROSE Oskar is a good preacher, Doctor von Zahnd. (*She blushes.*) My boys.

DOCTOR VON ZAHND Hello, boys.

THE THREE BOYS Hello, Doctor.

The youngest has picked something up from the floor.

JÖRG–LUKAS   A lamp cord, Doctor. It was lying on the floor.

DOCTOR VON ZAHND   Thank you, young man. Marvelous boys, Mrs. Rose. You have good reason to trust in the future.

Mrs. Rose sits down on the sofa to the right, Doctor von Zahnd at the table left. Behind the sofa the three boys, and on the armchair on the far right, Mr. Rose.

MRS. ROSE   Doctor, I have brought my boys with me for a reason. Oskar is taking over a mission in the Marianas.

MR. ROSE   In the Pacific Ocean.

MRS. ROSE   And I thought it proper that my boys should make their father's acquaintance before we leave. For the first and last time. They were still small when he fell ill, and now, perhaps, they will be saying good-bye forever.

DOCTOR VON ZAHND   Mrs. Rose, medically speaking, I may have some scruples, but as a human being I sympathize with your wish and gladly give my consent to this family reunion.

MRS. ROSE   How is my sweet little Johann Wilhelm?

DOCTOR VON ZAHND (*leafing through the file*)   Our dear Möbius is showing no signs of either improvement or relapse, Mrs. Rose. He spins a cocoon around himself, a world of his own.

MRS. ROSE   Does he still claim to see King Solomon?

DOCTOR VON ZAHND   Yes.

MR. ROSE   A sad, lamentable delusion.

DOCTOR VON ZAHND   Your stern judgment surprises me a little, Mr. Rose. Surely, as a theologian you must reckon with the possibility of a miracle.

MR. ROSE Of course—but not in the case of a mental patient.

DOCTOR VON ZAHND Whether the appearances perceived by the mentally ill are real or not is something that psychiatry is not competent to judge, my dear Mr. Rose. Psychiatry has to concern itself exclusively with the condition of the mind and the nerves, and in this respect our dear Mr. Möbius is in a sad condition indeed, even though the illness is taking a mild course. How to help him? My God! Another course of insulin shock treatment might have been called for, I won't deny it, but since none of the others made any difference, I left well enough alone. I am unfortunately not a magician, Mrs. Rose, and I can't coddle our dear old Möbius back to health, but I don't want to torment him either.

MRS. ROSE Does he know that I got—I mean, does he know about the divorce?

DOCTOR VON ZAHND He has been informed.

MRS. ROSE Did he understand?

DOCTOR VON ZAHND He takes hardly any interest in the outside world any more.

MRS. ROSE Doctor. Try to understand my situation. When I first met him, he was a fifteen-year-old schoolboy. He had rented an attic room in my father's house. He was an orphan and miserably poor. I made it possible for him to enter college and later to study physics. We got married on his twentieth birthday. Against my parents' wishes. We worked day and night. He was writing his dissertation, and I took a job with a shipping company. Four years later we had our oldest son, Adolf-Friedrich, and then the two other boys. Finally there were prospects of a professorship, and we thought we could finally breathe freely. But then Johann Wilhelm fell ill, and his sickness swallowed up huge amounts of money. To provide for my family, I went to work in a chocolate factory. Tobler's Chocolate. (*She silently wipes away a tear.*)   My whole life has been a struggle.

All are moved.

DOCTOR VON ZAHND   Mrs. Rose, you are a courageous woman.

MR. ROSE   And a good mother.

MRS. ROSE   Doctor. Up till now I have made it possible for Johann Wilhelm to stay in your sanatorium. The fees were far beyond my means, but God always came to my aid. However, now I am financially depleted. I can no longer raise the additional money.

DOCTOR VON ZAHND   That's understandable, Mrs. Rose.

MRS. ROSE   I'm afraid now you'll think I just married Oskar so I would no longer have to provide for Johann Wilhelm. But that's not the case. Things are even harder for me now. Oskar is bringing six boys into our marriage.

DOCTOR VON ZAHND   Six?

MR. ROSE   Six.

MRS. ROSE   Six. Oskar is a passionate father. But now there are nine children to feed, and Oskar is by no means robust, and he earns a meager salary. (*She cries.*)

DOCTOR VON ZAHND   Now, now, Mrs. Rose. Don't cry.

MRS. ROSE   I reproach myself bitterly for having left my poor little Johann Wilhelm in the lurch.

DOCTOR VON ZAHND   Mrs. Rose! You don't need to reproach yourself.

MRS. ROSE   My sweet little Johann Wilhelm will probably be interned in a state hospital now.

DOCTOR VON ZAHND   No he won't, Mrs.Rose. Our dear old Möbius will stay on here in the villa. You have my word. He has gotten used to living here and has found some nice, dear colleagues. I'm not a monster, you know.

MRS. ROSE   You are so good to me, Doctor.

DOCTOR VON ZAHND   Not at all, Mrs.Rose. It's just that there are such things as endowments. The Oppel Foundation for Ailing Scientists, the Doctor Steinmann Endowment. There's money lying around like hay, and it is my duty as a doctor to pitch some of it in the direction of your little Johann Wilhelm. You can steam off to the Marianas with a good conscience. But now let us bring in our dear old Möbius.

She goes upstage and opens door number one. Mrs. Rose rises, agitated.

DOCTOR VON ZAHND (*cont.*)   Dear Möbius. You have visitors. Leave your physicist's den for a moment and come in here.

Johann Wilhelm Möbius comes out of room number one, a forty-year-old, rather awkward man. He looks around uncertainly, scrutinizes Mrs. Rose, then the boys, and finally the missionary with apparent incomprehension, and remains silent.

MRS. ROSE   Johann Wilhelm.

THE BOYS   Daddy.

Möbius remains silent.

DOCTOR VON ZAHND   My dear Möbius, I should hope you can still recognize your wife.

MÖBIUS (*staring at Mrs. Rose*)   Lina?

DOCTOR VON ZAHND There's a glimmer after all, Möbius. Of course it's your Lina.

MÖBIUS Hello, Lina.

MRS. ROSE My sweet little Johann Wilhelm, my dear, dear little Johann Wilhelm.

DOCTOR VON ZAHND Well, there we are. Mrs. Rose, Mr. Rose, if you have anything further to discuss with me, I am at your disposal in the new wing over there. (*She exits through the french door left.*)

MRS. ROSE Your boys, Johann Wilhelm.

MÖBIUS (*taken aback*) Three?

MRS. ROSE But of course, Johann Wilhelm. Three. (*She introduces the boys to him.*) Adolf-Friedrich, your eldest.

Möbius shakes the boy's hand.

MÖBIUS Nice to see you, Adolf-Friedrich, my eldest.

ADOLF-FRIEDRICH Hello, Daddy.

MÖBIUS How old are you, Adolf-Friedrich?

ADOLF-FRIEDRICH Sixteen, Daddy.

MÖBIUS What do you want to be?

ADOLF-FRIEDRICH A minister, Daddy.

MÖBIUS I remember. We were walking across the Josefsplatz. I was holding your hand. The sun was very bright and the shadows looked as if they had been drawn with a compass. (*Turning to the next boy.*) And you—you are?

WILFRIED-KASPAR My name is Wilfried-Kaspar, Daddy.

MÖBIUS Fourteen?

26

WILFRIED-KASPAR   Fifteen. I want to study philosophy.

MÖBIUS   Philosophy?

MRS. ROSE   An exceptionally precocious child.

WILFRIED-KASPAR   I have read Schopenhauer and Nietzsche.

MRS. ROSE   Your youngest, Jörg-Lukas. Fourteen.

JÖRG-LUKAS   Hello, Daddy.

MÖBIUS   Hello, Jörg-Lukas, my youngest.

MRS. ROSE   He's the one who most resembles you.

JÖRG-LUKAS   I want to be a physicist, Daddy.

MÖBIUS (*stares at his youngest with alarm*)   A physicist?

JÖRG-LUKAS   Yes, Daddy.

MÖBIUS   You mustn't, Jörg-Lukas. Not under any circumstances. Get this out of your head. I—I forbid it.

JÖRG-LUKAS (*confused*)   But you became a physicist, Daddy—

MÖBIUS   I should never have done that, Jörg-Lukas. Never. I wouldn't be in a madhouse now.

MRS. ROSE   But Johann Wilhelm, you're mistaken. You're in a sanatorium, not a madhouse. You have some trouble with your nerves, that's all.

MÖBIUS (*shaking his head*)   No, Lina. People consider me crazy. Everyone. You too. And my boys too. Because King Solomon appears to me.

All fall silent with embarrassment. Mrs. Rose introduces Mr. Rose.

MRS. ROSE   Let me introduce Oskar Rose to you, Johann Wilhelm. My husband. He is a missionary.

27

MÖBIUS   Your husband? But I'm your husband.

MRS. ROSE   Not any more, my dear little Johann Wilhelm. (*She blushes.*)   We're divorced, remember?

MÖBIUS   Divorced?

MRS. ROSE   But you know that.

MÖBIUS   No, I don't.

MRS. ROSE   Doctor von Zahnd told you. Definitely.

MÖBIUS   Possibly.

MRS. ROSE   And so then I married Oskar. He has six boys. He was a minister in Guttannen and now he has accepted a post in the Marianas.

MR. ROSE   In the Pacific Ocean.

MRS. ROSE   We're sailing from Bremen the day after tomorrow.

Möbius remains silent. The others are embarrassed.

MRS. ROSE (*cont.*)   Yes. That's how it is.

MÖBIUS (*nodding at Mr. Rose*)   I'm pleased to meet the new father of my boys.

MR. ROSE   I have taken them into my heart, Mr. Möbius, all three of them. God will provide. As the psalmist says: the Lord is my shepherd, I shall not want.

MRS. ROSE   Oskar knows all the psalms by heart. The psalms of David, the psalms of Solomon.

MÖBIUS   I'm glad the boys have found a responsible father. I was an inadequate father to them.

MRS. ROSE But Johann Wilhelm.

MÖBIUS I congratulate you from the bottom of my heart.

MRS. ROSE It's time for us to leave.

MÖBIUS For the Marianas.

MRS. ROSE To say good-bye.

MÖBIUS Forever.

MRS. ROSE Your boys are remarkably musical, Johann Wilhelm. They show a real talent on the recorder. Play something for your Daddy, boys, as a farewell gift.

THE BOYS Yes, Mommy.

Adolf-Friedrich opens the briefcase and distributes the recorders.

MRS. ROSE Have a seat, my dear little Johann Wilhelm.

Möbius sits down at the round table. Mrs. Rose and Mr. Rose sit down on the couch. The boys take their positions in the middle of the room.

JÖRG-LUKAS Something by Boxtehude.

ADOLF-FRIEDRICH One, two, three.

The boys play.

MRS. ROSE With more feeling, boys, more tenderly.

The boys play more tenderly. Möbius jumps up.

MÖBIUS Please don't! Please, that's enough!

The boys stop playing, bewildered.

MÖBIUS (*cont.*) Don't play any more. Please. For Solomon's sake. Don't play any more.

MRS. ROSE   But Johann Wilhelm!

MÖBIUS   Please, no more music. No more music, please. Please, please.

MR. ROSE   Mr. Möbius. King Solomon more than anyone will be gladdened by the piping of these innocent boys. Just think: Solomon, the psalmist, the singer of the Song of Songs!

MÖBIUS   Mr. Rose. I have met Solomon face to face. He is no longer the great golden king who sings of the Shulamite and of the young roes that are twins, which feed among the lilies. He has cast away his purple robe—

Suddenly Möbius rushes past his horrified family to his room and throws open the door.

MÖBIUS (*cont.*)   —naked and stinking he cowers in my room as the poor King of Truth, and his psalms are terrible. Listen well, missionary, you love the psalms, you know them all, commit these to memory as well:

He has gone to the round table left, turns it over, climbs into it, and sits down.

MÖBIUS (*cont.*)
A psalm of Solomon to be sung to the Cosmonauts.
We hightailed it to outer space.
To the deserts of the moon.
Foundered in their dust.
Some kicked the bucket right there
Without a sound. But most of us
Were boiled in the lead fumes of Mercury,
Dissolved in the oil swamps of Venus, and
Even on Mars we were food for the sun,
Thundering, radioactive, and yellow.

MRS. ROSE   But Johann Wilhelm—

MÖBIUS

Jupiter stank,
An arrow-swift rotating methane pulp,
It hovered above us, so overpowering
We puked all over Ganymede.

MR. ROSE   Mr. Möbius—

MÖBIUS

Saturn we greeted with curses.
What came after that is not worth mentioning:
Uranus, Neptune,
A glaze of gray-green ice.
Over Pluto and Transpluto fell
The last dirty jokes.

THE BOYS   Daddy—

MÖBIUS

For we had long since mistaken the sun for Sirius,
Sirius for Canopus.
Drifted off course, we drove into the deep
Toward a few white stars,
Which we never reached anyhow,

MRS. ROSE   Johann Wilhelm! My dear little Johann Wilhelm!

MÖBIUS

Long since mummified in our spacecraft,
Caked with filth.

The Head Nurse enters from the right with NURSE MONIKA.

HEAD NURSE   But Mr. Möbius.

MÖBIUS
　　In our grinning skulls no memory
　　Of the breathing Earth.

He sits rigidly, his face like a mask, inside the upended table.

MRS. ROSE　My dear little Johann Wilhelm—

MÖBIUS　Off with you! To the Marianas!

THE BOYS　Daddy!

MÖBIUS　Off with you! Beat it! To the Marianas! (*He rises menacingly. The Rose family is confused.*)

HEAD NURSE　Come, Mrs. Rose, come, boys, and you, Mr. Rose. He has to calm down, that's all.

MÖBIUS　Out with you! Out!

HEAD NURSE　A slight attack. Monika will stay with him, she'll calm him down. A slight attack.

MÖBIUS　Scram, the lot of you! Forever! To the Pacific Ocean!

JÖRG-LUKAS　Good-bye, Daddy! Good-bye!

The Head Nurse leads the distressed and weeping family off to the right. Möbius yells after them without restraint.

MÖBIUS　I never want to see you again! You have insulted King Solomon! May you be damned forever! May you and all the Marianas drown in the Mariana Deep! Six thousand fathoms down! May you rot in the darkest hole of the sea, forgotten by God and man!

NURSE MONIKA　We are alone. Your family can no longer hear you.

Möbius stares wonderingly at Nurse Monika and finally seems to recover his senses.

MÖBIUS Oh, of course.

Nurse Monika is silent. He is somewhat embarrassed.

MÖBIUS (*cont.*) I guess I was a little agitated.

NURSE MONIKA Quite.

MÖBIUS I had to say the truth.

NURSE MONIKA Obviously.

MÖBIUS I got upset.

NURSE MONIKA You put on an act.

MÖBIUS You see through me?

NURSE MONIKA I've been taking care of you for two years.

MÖBIUS (*paces up and down and then stops.*) Fine. I admit it. I was pretending to be crazy.

NURSE MONIKA Why?

MÖBIUS To take leave of my wife and my sons. Forever.

NURSE MONIKA In this horrible way?

MÖBIUS In this humane way. If you're already in a madhouse, the best way to wipe out the past is to behave like a madman. My family can now forget me with a clear conscience. After my performance, they'll never want to visit me again. The consequences for myself are unimportant; all that matters is the life that goes on outside. Madness is expensive. For fifteen years my Lina has been paying monstrous sums. I had to put a stop to it. The time was right. Solomon revealed to me what there was to be

33

revealed, the System of All Possible Inventions has been completed, the last pages have been dictated, and my wife has found a new husband, a missionary, decent to his bones. You can relax now, Nurse. Everything is all right. (*He is about to exit.*)

NURSE MONIKA   You plan your actions.

MÖBIUS   I am a physicist. (*He turns to go to his room.*)

NURSE MONIKA   Mr. Möbius.

MÖBIUS (*stops*)   Yes, Nurse?

NURSE MONIKA   I have to talk to you.

MÖBIUS   Go ahead.

NURSE MONIKA   It's about the two of us.

MÖBIUS   Let's sit down.

They sit down. She on the sofa, he in the armchair on its left.

NURSE MONIKA   We too must take leave of each other. Also forever.

MÖBIUS (*frightened*)   You're leaving me?

NURSE MONIKA   Orders from above.

MÖBIUS   What happened?

NURSE MONIKA   I'm being transferred to the main building. Tomorrow the patients here will be supervised by male nurses. No female nurses will be allowed to enter the villa any more.

MÖBIUS   Because of Newton and Einstein?

NURSE MONIKA   At the request of the district attorney. Doctor von Zahnd was afraid there would be trouble and gave in.

Silence.

MÖBIUS (*dejected*) Monika, I am an awkward person. I have forgotten how to express my feelings. Talking shop with the two sick men I live with can hardly be called conversation. I'm afraid I've become mute inside as well. But I want you to know that for me everything has changed since I've known you. It's more bearable. Well, now that time is over too. For two years I was a little happier than usual. Because through you, Monika, I found the courage to accept my isolation, my fate as—as a madman. Farewell. (*He stands up and holds out his hand.*)

NURSE MONIKA Mr. Möbius, I don't believe you're—a madman.

MÖBIUS (*laughs, sits down again*) Neither do I. But that doesn't change my position in any way. It's my bad luck that King Solomon keeps appearing to me. The fact is, there's nothing more scandalous than a miracle in the realm of science.

NURSE MONIKA Mr. Möbius, I believe in this miracle.

MÖBIUS (*stares at her dumbfounded*) You believe?

NURSE MONIKA In King Solomon.

MÖBIUS That he appears to me?

NURSE MONIKA That he appears to you.

MÖBIUS Every day, every night?

NURSE MONIKA Every day, every night.

MÖBIUS That he dictates the secrets of nature to me? The interconnectedness of all things? The System of All Possible Inventions?

35

NURSE MONIKA   I believe it all. And if you told me that King David also appeared to you with all his retinue, I would believe it. I simply know that you're not sick. I feel it.

Silence. Then Möbius leaps to his feet.

MÖBIUS   Monika! Leave now!

NURSE MONIKA (*remains seated*)   I'm staying.

MÖBIUS   I never want to see you again.

NURSE MONIKA   You need me. You have no one else in the world. Not a soul.

MÖBIUS   It is fatal to believe in King Solomon.

NURSE MONIKA   I love you.

Perplexed, Möbius stares at Monika, and sits down again. Silence.

MÖBIUS (*softly, dejectedly*)   You're headed for disaster.

NURSE MONIKA   I'm not afraid for myself, I'm afraid for you. Newton and Einstein are dangerous.

MÖBIUS   I get along with them.

NURSE MONIKA   Dorothea and Irene got along with them too. And then they got killed.

MÖBIUS   Monika. You have confessed your faith and your love to me. You're forcing me to tell you the truth as well. I, too, love you, Monika.

She stares at him.

MÖBIUS (*cont.*)   More than my life. And that is why you are in danger. Because we love each other.

Einstein comes out of room number two, smoking a pipe.

EINSTEIN   I woke up again.

NURSE MONIKA   Now, now, Professor.

EINSTEIN   I suddenly remembered.

NURSE MONIKA   Come now, Professor.

EINSTEIN   I strangled Irene.

NURSE MONIKA   Forget about it, Professor.

EINSTEIN (*looking at his hands*)   Will I ever be able to play the violin again?

Möbius stands up as if to protect Monika.

MÖBIUS   You were playing just a while ago.

EINSTEIN   Reasonably well?

MÖBIUS   The Kreutzer Sonata. While the police were here.

EINSTEIN   The Kreutzer Sonata. Thank God. (*His face, after lighting up, turns somber again.*)   And yet I don't like playing the violin, and I don't like this pipe either. It tastes awful.

MÖBIUS   So give it up.

EINSTEIN   I can't do that. I'm Albert Einstein (*He gives both of them a sharp look.*)   Are you two in love?

NURSE MONIKA   We're in love.

Einstein thoughtfully goes upstage to where the murdered nurse lay and looks at the chalk drawing on the floor

EINSTEIN   Irene and I were also in love. She wanted to do everything for me, Irene did. I warned her. I yelled at her. I treated her like a dog. I begged her to run away. In vain. She stayed. She wanted to move to the country with me.

37

To Kohlwang. She wanted to marry me. She had even obtained permission for the wedding. From Doctor von Zahnd. Then I strangled her. Poor Irene. There is nothing more absurd on the face of the earth than women's frantic urge to sacrifice themselves.

NURSE MONIKA (*goes to him*)   Go and lie down again, Professor.

EINSTEIN   You may call me Albert.

NURSE MONIKA   Be sensible, Albert.

EINSTEIN   You be sensible yourself, Monika. Listen to the man you love and flee from him! Otherwise you're lost. (*He turns back toward room number two.*)   I'm going back to sleep. (*He disappears into room number two.*)

NURSE MONIKA   Poor deluded man.

MÖBIUS   He should have finally convinced you of the impossibility of loving me.

NURSE MONIKA   You are not insane.

MÖBIUS   It would be more rational if you considered me insane. Escape! Get lost! Beat it! Or I'll treat you like a dog myself.

NURSE MONIKA   Why don't you treat me like a lover?

MÖBIUS   Come here, Monika. (*He leads her to an armchair, sits down facing her, and takes her hands.*)   Listen. I made a serious mistake. I revealed my secret, I didn't keep King Solomon's visits to myself. He's making me suffer for it. For the rest of my life. That's all right. But you shouldn't be punished for that as well. In the eyes of the world, you are in love with a lunatic. This can only have tragic consequences. Leave this sanatorium, forget me. That will be the best thing for both of us.

NURSE MONIKA Do you want me?

MÖBIUS Why do you talk like that?

NURSE MONIKA I want to sleep with you, I want to have children with you. I know, I sound shameless. But why don't you look at me? Do you find me unattractive? I know this outfit is hideous. (*She tears off her nurse's cap.*) I hate my profession! For five years I've been tending to the sick, in the name of charity. I never flinched; I was there for everyone; I sacrificed myself. But now I want to sacrifice myself for one person alone, to be there for one person alone, not always for others. I want to be there for the man I love. For you. I will do anything you ask of me, I'll work for you day and night, just don't send me away! I don't have anyone in the world except you, either! I'm alone too!

MÖBIUS Monika, I have to send you away.

NURSE MONIKA (*desperately*) Don't you love me at all?

MÖBIUS I do love you, Monika. My God, I love you, that's the insanity.

NURSE MONIKA Then why do you deny me? And not only me. You claim that King Solomon appears to you. Why do you deny him too?

MÖBIUS (*extremely agitated, grabbing her*) Monika! You can believe anything about me, call me a weakling. That's your right. I am unworthy of your love. But I have remained faithful to King Solomon. He burst into my life, suddenly, unbidden, he abused me, he destroyed my life, but I did not deny him.

NURSE MONIKA Are you sure?

MÖBIUS You doubt it?

NURSE MONIKA You think you have to atone because you did not keep his appearances secret. But maybe you are atoning because you don't make his revelation known to the world.

MÖBIUS (*letting go of her*) I—I don't understand.

NURSE MONIKA He dictates to you the System of All Possible Inventions. Are you fighting for its recognition?

MÖBIUS But I'm supposed to be insane.

NURSE MONIKA Why so little courage?

MÖBIUS In my case, courage is a crime.

NURSE MONIKA Johann Wilhelm. I talked to Doctor von Zahnd.

MÖBIUS (*staring at her*) You talked?

NURSE MONIKA You are free.

MÖBIUS Free?

NURSE MONIKA We can get married.

MÖBIUS My God.

NURSE MONIKA Doctor von Zahnd has already made all the arrangements. She still considers you a sick man, but not dangerous. And not genetically defective. She said she was crazier than you are, and laughed.

MÖBIUS That's nice of her.

NURSE MONIKA Isn't she a wonderful human being?

MÖBIUS Absolutely.

NURSE MONIKA   Johann Wilhelm! I have accepted a post as district nurse in Blumenstein. I've been saving. We have nothing to worry about. All we need to do is love each other.

Möbius has risen. It gradually gets darker in the room.

NURSE MONIKA *(cont.)*   Isn't that wonderful?

MÖBIUS   Absolutely.

NURSE MONIKA   You don't sound very happy.

MÖBIUS   It's all so unexpected.

NURSE MONIKA   I've done even more.

MÖBIUS   What would that be?

NURSE MONIKA   I spoke to the famous physicist Professor Scherbert.

MÖBIUS   He was my teacher.

NURSE MONIKA   He remembered you perfectly. He said you were his best student.

MÖBIUS   And what did you discuss with him?

NURSE MONIKA   He promised he would examine your manuscripts with an open mind.

MÖBIUS   Did you make it clear that they come from King Solomon?

NURSE MONIKA   Of course.

MÖBIUS   And?

NURSE MONIKA   He laughed. He said you always had a wild sense of humor. Johann Wilhelm! We mustn't only think of ourselves. You have been chosen. King Solomon has

41

appeared to you, revealed himself in all his glory. You have partaken of the wisdom of heaven. Now you must walk the path ordained by that miracle, and stay on that path even if it leads through mockery and laughter, through disbelief and doubt. But that way leads out of this asylum. Johann Wilhelm, it leads to public recognition, not to solitude. It leads into battle. I am there to help you, to fight by your side. The heavens that sent you King Solomon sent me too.

Möbius stares out of the window.

NURSE MONIKA (*cont.*)   Dearest.

MÖBIUS   My love?

NURSE MONIKA   Aren't you happy?

MÖBIUS   Very.

NURSE MONIKA   Now we must pack your bags. The train is leaving at eight twenty. To Blumenstein. (*She goes to room number one.*)

MÖBIUS (*alone*)   There isn't much.

Monika comes out of room number one with a stack of manuscripts.

NURSE MONIKA   Your manuscripts. (*Puts them on the table.*) It's gotten dark.

MÖBIUS   It gets dark early these days.

NURSE MONIKA   I'll turn on the light. Then I'll pack your bags.

MÖBIUS   Wait a moment. Come to me.

She goes to him. Only their silhouettes are visible.

NURSE MONIKA   You have tears in your eyes.

MÖBIUS You too.

NURSE MONIKA Tears of happiness.

He tears down the curtain and throws it over her. A brief struggle. The silhouettes are no longer visible. Then silence. The door of room number three opens. A ray of light penetrates into the room. In the doorway stands Newton in a costume of his century. Möbius goes to the table, picks up the manuscripts.

NEWTON What happened?

MÖBIUS (*goes to his room*) I strangled Monika Stettler.

The sound of Einstein playing his violin is heard from room number two.

NEWTON Einstein's at it again. Kreisler. "Schön Rosmarin." (*He goes to the fireplace and takes out the cognac.*)

ACT TWO

An hour later, the same room. It is night outside. The police again. More measuring, recording, photographing. Except this time the body of Monika Stettler, invisible to the audience, is presumed to be lying beneath the window upstage right. The drawing room is lit. The chandelier and the floor lamp have been switched on. On the sofa sits Doctor Mathilde von Zahnd, looking gloomy and preoccupied. On the little table before her, a box of cigars. Guhl, with his stenographer's pad, sits in the armchair on the far right. Inspector Voss, wearing a coat and a hat, turns away from the corpse and comes downstage.

DOCTOR VON ZAHND   A Havana?

INSPECTOR   No, thanks.

DOCTOR VON ZAHND   Schnapps?

INSPECTOR   Later.

Silence.

INSPECTOR (*cont.*)   Blocher, you can take the pictures now.

BLOCHER   Yes, sir.

Photographs are taken. Flashes.

INSPECTOR   What was the nurse's name?

DOCTOR VON ZAHND   Monika Stettler.

INSPECTOR   Age?

DOCTOR VON ZAHND   Twenty-five. From Blumenstein.

INSPECTOR   Relatives?

44

DOCTOR VON ZAHND   None.

INSPECTOR   Did you get her statement, Blocher?

BLOCHER   Yes, I did, Inspector.

INSPECTOR   Strangled again, Doctor?

MEDICAL EXAMINER   No doubt about it. Once again with tremendous force. But this time with the curtain cord.

INSPECTOR   Just like three months ago. (*Wearily, he sits down in the armchair downstage right.*)

DOCTOR VON ZAHND   Would you like to have the murderer—

INSPECTOR   Please, Doctor.

DOCTOR VON ZAHND   I mean, the perpetrator brought in?

INSPECTOR   I wouldn't think of it.

DOCTOR VON ZAHND   But—

INSPECTOR   Doctor von Zahnd. I do my duty, I take down evidence, I examine the corpse, I have it photographed and submitted to a forensic examination, but I will not examine Möbius. I leave him to you. For good. Along with the other radioactive physicists.

DOCTOR VON ZAHND   And the district attorney?

INSPECTOR   He's beyond rage. He's brooding.

DOCTOR VON ZAHND (*wiping sweat from her brow*)   It's hot in here.

INSPECTOR   Not at all.

DOCTOR VON ZAHND   This third murder—

INSPECTOR Please, Doctor.

DOCTOR VON ZAHND This third accident is all I needed in Les Cerisiers. I might as well resign. Monika Stettler was my best nurse. She understood the mental patients. She had empathy. I loved her like a daughter. But her death is not the worst of it. My reputation as a doctor is ruined.

INSPECTOR It'll come back. Blocher, take another shot from above.

BLOCHER Yes, Inspector.

From the right, two huge male nurses roll in a cart with food, plates, and cutlery. One of the nurses is a black man. They are accompanied by an equally gigantic chief male nurse, UWE SIEVERS.

UWE SIEVERS Dinner for our dear patients, Doctor.

INSPECTOR *(leaps to his feet)* Uwe Sievers.

UWE SIEVERS That's right, Inspector. Uwe Sievers. Former European heavyweight boxing champion. Now head nurse at Les Cerisiers.

INSPECTOR And those two other monsters?

UWE SIEVERS Murillo, South American champion, also heavyweight, and McArthur (*He points at the black man.*) North American champion, middleweight. The table, McArthur.

McARTHUR *sets the overturned table on its feet.*

UWE SIEVERS The tablecloth, Murillo.

MURILLO *spreads a white cloth over the table.*

UWE SIEVERS The Meissen china, McArthur.

McArthur distributes the plates.

UWE SIEVERS The silver, Murillo.

Murillo lays out the silver.

UWE SIEVERS The soup tureen in the middle, McArthur.

McArthur sets the soup tureen on the table.

INSPECTOR And what are the dear patients having for dinner? (*He lifts the lid of the tureen.*) Liver dumpling soup.

UWE SIEVERS Poulet à la broche, cordon bleu.

INSPECTOR Fantastic.

UWE SIEVERS First class.

INSPECTOR I'm a fourteenth-class civil servant. Basic home cooking, that's what I'm used to.

UWE SIEVERS Dinner is served, Doctor von Zahnd.

DOCTOR VON ZAHND You may leave, Sievers. The patients will help themselves.

UWE SIEVERS Inspector, it was an honor meeting you.

The three male nurses bow and exit right.

INSPECTOR (*gazing after them*) That's really something.

DOCTOR VON ZAHND Satisfied?

INSPECTOR Envious. If we had them in the police force—

DOCTOR VON ZAHND Their wages are astronomical.

INSPECTOR With your industrial barons and multimillion-airesses you can afford it. Those fellows will finally put the district attorney's mind at rest. No one's going to slip through *their* fingers.

Einstein can be heard playing his violin in room number two.

DOCTOR VON ZAHND   The Kreutzer Sonata again.

INSPECTOR   I know. The andante.

BLOCHER   We're finished, Inspector.

INSPECTOR   Then take the body out, as usual.

The two policemen pick up the corpse. Möbius rushes out of room number one.

MÖBIUS   Monika! My love!

The policemen stand still, holding the corpse. Doctor von Zahnd rises majestically.

DOCTOR VON ZAHND   Möbius! How could you! You have killed my best nurse, my gentlest nurse, my sweetest nurse!

MÖBIUS   I'm so sorry, Doctor von Zahnd.

DOCTOR VON ZAHND   Sorry.

MÖBIUS   King Solomon commanded me to do it.

DOCTOR VON ZAHND   King Solomon . . . (*She sits down. Heavily. Pale.*)   His Majesty gave the orders for the murder.

MÖBIUS   I was standing by the window gazing into the darkening dusk. Then the King came floating up from the park over the terrace, right up to me, very close, and whispered his order through the windowpane.

DOCTOR VON ZAHND   Excuse me, Voss. My nerves.

INSPECTOR   That's quite all right.

DOCTOR VON ZAHND   A place like this can really wear you out.

INSPECTOR   I can imagine.

48

DOCTOR VON ZAHND   I'm going to withdraw now. (*She stands up.*)   Inspector Voss, please convey to the district attorney my profound regret for the incidents in my sanatorium. Please assure him that everything is in control again. Doctor, gentlemen, it was an honor. (*She first goes upstage left, bows ceremoniously to the corpse, then looks at Möbius and exits right.*)

INSPECTOR   All right. Now you can finally take the body to the chapel. Next to the other nurse, Irene.

MÖBIUS   Monika!

The two policemen with the corpse and the others carrying the technical gear go out through the door to the park. The forensic doctor follows.

MÖBIUS (*cont.*)   My beloved Monika.

INSPECTOR (*walks up to the small table beside the sofa*)   Now I really have to have a Havana. I've earned it. (*Takes a huge cigar from the box, looks at it.*)   Quite something. (*Bites off the end, lights the cigar.*)   My dear Möbius, hidden away behind the fire screen you'll find Sir Isaac Newton's cognac.

MÖBIUS   Gladly, Inspector.

The Inspector puffs away while Möbius fetches the glass and the bottle of cognac.

MÖBIUS (*cont.*)   May I pour you a glass?

INSPECTOR   You may. (*He takes the glass, drinks.*)

MÖBIUS   Another one?

INSPECTOR   Another one.

MÖBIUS (*pouring another glass*)   Inspector, I must ask you to arrest me.

INSPECTOR   But what ever for, my dear Möbius?

MÖBIUS   Well, on account of that nurse, Monika—

INSPECTOR   According to your own confession you were acting on orders from King Solomon. As long as I'm unable to arrest him, you're a free man.

MÖBIUS   Still—

INSPECTOR   Still nothing. Pour me another one.

MÖBIUS   All right, Inspector.

INSPECTOR   But now put the bottle away, otherwise those male nurses will polish it off.

MÖBIUS   Yes, sir. (*He hides the cognac.*)

INSPECTOR   Sit down.

MÖBIUS   Yes, sir. (*Sits down on the chair.*)

INSPECTOR   Over here. (*Pointing at the sofa.*)

MÖBIUS   Yes, sir. (*Sits down on the sofa.*)

INSPECTOR   You see, every year in this small town and the surrounding district, I arrest a few murderers. Not many. Barely half a dozen. Some of them I arrest with pleasure, others I feel sorry for. But I have to arrest them regardless. Justice is justice. And now you come along, you and your two colleagues. At first I was angry, because my hands were tied. But now? Suddenly I'm enjoying it. I could shout with joy. I have found three murderers whom I can leave scot-free, and I can do that with a good conscience. For the first time, justice is on holiday, which is a tremendous feeling. Serving justice is a terrific strain, my friend, it wears you out, physically and morally. I simply need a break. And it's to you, my good fellow, that I owe this pleasure. Good-bye. Give my kind regards to Newton and Einstein, and my respects to King Solomon.

MÖBIUS   Yes, sir.

The Inspector exits. Möbius is alone. He sits down on the sofa and presses his hands against his temples. Newton comes out of room number three.

NEWTON   What's for dinner?

Möbius does not reply.

NEWTON (*cont.*) (*lifts the lid off the tureen*)   Liver dumpling soup. (*Lifts the lids off the other dishes on the cart.*)   Poulet à la broche, cordon bleu. That's strange. Usually we have a light dinner. And nothing fancy. Ever since the other patients were moved into the new building. (*He ladles some soup into his dish.*)   No appetite?

Möbius remains silent.

NEWTON (*cont.*)   I understand. After my nurse I lost my appetite too.

He sits down and starts eating liver dumpling soup. Möbius rises and is about to go into his room.

NEWTON (*cont.*)   Stay.

MÖBIUS   Yes, Sir Isaac?

NEWTON   There's something I have to discuss with you, Möbius.

MÖBIUS (*remains standing*)   Yes?

NEWTON (*indicating the food*)   Wouldn't you like to try the liver dumpling soup after all? It's delicious.

MÖBIUS   No.

NEWTON My dear Möbius, we are no longer in the care of female nurses, we are being guarded by male nurses. Huge brawny fellows.

MÖBIUS Makes no difference to me.

NEWTON Maybe not to you, Möbius. You obviously prefer to spend your whole life in a madhouse. But to me it makes a difference. Because I want out. (*He finishes the liver dumpling soup.*) Well. Now for the poulet à la broche. (*He helps himself.*) The male nurses are forcing me to take action. Before the day is over.

MÖBIUS That's your business.

NEWTON Not entirely. Here's a confession, Möbius: I'm not crazy.

MÖBIUS Of course not, Sir Isaac.

NEWTON I am not Sir Isaac Newton.

MÖBIUS I know. You're Albert Einstein.

NEWTON Nonsense. Nor am I the Herbert Georg Beutler I'm presumed to be around here. My real name is Kilton, my friend.

MÖBIUS (*stares at him with alarm*) Alec Jasper Kilton?

NEWTON Correct.

MÖBIUS The creator of the Theory of Equivalence?

NEWTON Precisely.

MÖBIUS (*approaching the table*) You sneaked in here?

NEWTON By pretending to be mad.

MÖBIUS In order to—spy on me?

NEWTON In order to get to the root of your madness. As for my impeccable German, I learned it in our secret service training camp. Horrendous drudgery.

MÖBIUS And because that poor nurse, Dorothea, stumbled on the truth, you—

NEWTON Yes. I greatly regret the incident.

MÖBIUS I understand.

NEWTON Orders are orders.

MÖBIUS Obviously.

NEWTON I couldn't have acted in any other way.

MÖBIUS Of course not.

NEWTON My mission was at stake, the most secret project of our secret service. I had to kill if I wanted to avoid suspicion. Nurse Dorothea no longer thought I was crazy, and the head psychiatrist thought I was just moderately ill. To prove my insanity once and for all, a murder was necessary. You know, this poulet à la broche is really superb.

Einstein can be heard fiddling in room number two.

MÖBIUS Einstein's fiddling again.

NEWTON The Bach Gavotte.

MÖBIUS His meal's getting cold.

NEWTON Forget about that nut. Let him fiddle.

MÖBIUS Is this a threat?

NEWTON I have boundless respect for you. I would regret having to take serious action against you.

MÖBIUS   You have an assignment to kidnap me?

NEWTON   If our secret service proves to be justified in its suspicion.

MÖBIUS   Which is?

NEWTON   That you happen to be the most brilliant physicist of our time.

MÖBIUS   Kilton, I am a man with a serious nervous disorder, and that's it.

NEWTON   Our secret service is of a different opinion.

MÖBIUS   And what do *you* think of me?

NEWTON   I consider you the greatest physicist of all time, period.

MÖBIUS   And how did your secret service get on my trail?

NEWTON   Through me. By chance I read your dissertation on the foundations of a new physics. At first I thought it was some kind of whimsy. Then the scales fell from my eyes. I was confronted with the most extraordinary document in modern physics. I began to make inquiries about its author and found nothing. Thereupon I informed our secret service, and they did find something.

EINSTEIN   You were not the only one who read that dissertation, Kilton. (*He has emerged unnoticed from room number two, holding his bow, with his violin under his arm.*) Frankly, I'm not crazy either. May I introduce myself? I too am a physicist. Member of a secret service. But a somewhat different one. My name is Joseph Eisler.

MÖBIUS   The discoverer of the Eisler Effect?

EINSTEIN   Precisely.

NEWTON Disappeared in nineteen fifty.

EINSTEIN Voluntarily.

NEWTON (*suddenly holding a revolver in his hand*) Eisler, would you mind standing with your face against the wall?

EINSTEIN But of course. (*He saunters leisurely to the fireplace, lays his violin on the mantelpiece, and then suddenly turns around with a revolver in his hand.*) My dear Kilton. I suspect we both know how to handle these weapons, so we would want to avoid a duel, don't you think? I will gladly put away my Browning if you will do the same with your Colt.

NEWTON Agreed.

EINSTEIN Behind the fire screen, next to the cognac. In case our attendants suddenly show up.

NEWTON All right.

They both put their revolvers behind the fire screen.

EINSTEIN You've messed up my plans, Kilton. I thought you really were insane.

NEWTON If it's any comfort: I thought the same of you.

EINSTEIN All sorts of things went wrong. That business with Irene this afternoon, for example. She was getting suspicious, and thus signed her own death warrant. I deeply regret the whole incident.

MÖBIUS I understand.

EINSTEIN Orders are orders.

MÖBIUS Obviously.

EINSTEIN I couldn't have acted in any other way.

MÖBIUS Of course not.

EINSTEIN My mission was at stake, just like yours, the most secret project of *our* secret service. Shall we sit?

NEWTON Let's sit down.

He sits down on the left side of the table, Einstein on the right.

MÖBIUS Eisler, I presume that you, too, want to force me—

EINSTEIN Now, now, Möbius.

MÖBIUS —induce me to visit your country.

EINSTEIN We, too, consider you the greatest physicist of all time. But now I look forward to dinner. Worthy of a last meal, I'm sure. (*He ladles soup into his plate.*) Still no appetite, Möbius?

MÖBIUS Yes. Suddenly it's back. Now that you've found me out. (*He sits down between them at the table and ladles soup into his plate.*)

NEWTON Burgundy, Möbius?

MÖBIUS Please.

NEWTON (*pouring the wine*) I'm going to attack the cordon bleu.

MÖBIUS Don't hold back.

NEWTON Bon appétit.

EINSTEIN Bon appétit.

MÖBIUS Bon appétit.

They eat. The three male nurses enter right. Uwe Sievers is carrying a notebook.

UWE SIEVERS Patient Beutler!

NEWTON Here.

UWE SIEVERS Patient Ernesti!

EINSTEIN Here.

UWE SIEVERS Patient Möbius!

MÖBIUS Here.

UWE SIEVERS Head Nurse Sievers, Attendant Murillo, Attendant McArthur. (*He puts the notebook away.*) On the advisement of the authorities, certain security measures will be taken. Murillo, the bars.

Murillo lets down a metal grating over the window. The room now suddenly resembles a prison.

UWE SIEVERS (*cont.*) McArthur, lock it.

McArthur locks it.

UWE SIEVERS (*cont.*) Do the gentlemen have any further requests for the night? Patient Beutler?

NEWTON No.

UWE SIEVERS Patient Ernesti?

EINSTEIN No.

UWE SIEVERS Patient Möbius?

MÖBIUS No.

UWE SIEVERS Gentlemen, adieu and good night.

Exit the three male nurses. Silence.

EINSTEIN Beasts.

NEWTON They've got more of those bruisers lurking in the park. I've been watching them from my window for some time.

EINSTEIN (*rises and examines the grating*) Solid. With a special lock.

NEWTON (*goes to the door of his room, opens it, looks in*) There's a grating over my window, too. What are they, magicians? (*He opens the other two doors.*) Same goes for Eisler. And Möbius (*He goes to the door right.*) Locked.

He sits down again. So does Einstein.

EINSTEIN Prisoners.

NEWTON Logical. We and our nurses.

EINSTEIN We'll never get out of this madhouse now unless we coordinate our actions.

MÖBIUS But I don't want to escape.

EINSTEIN Möbius—

MÖBIUS I don't see the slightest reason why I should. On the contrary. I'm satisfied with my fate.

Silence.

NEWTON But I am not satisfied with it—a fairly crucial detail, wouldn't you say? With all due respect to your personal feelings, you are a genius, and as such, common property. You have opened up new horizons in physics. But you don't hold a patent on science. It is your duty to open the doors to us as well, the nongeniuses. Come with me, and within a year we'll put you in a tuxedo, transport you to Stockholm, and you will receive the Nobel Prize.

MÖBIUS Your secret service is altruistic.

NEWTON I'll tell you frankly, Möbius, what impresses them most is the possibility that you may have solved the problem of gravity.

MÖBIUS True.

Silence.

EINSTEIN You say that so calmly.

MÖBIUS How else should I say it?

EINSTEIN My secret service believed that you might discover the Unified Theory of Elementary Particles.

MÖBIUS Then I can set their minds at ease too. The Unified Field Theory has been discovered.

NEWTON (*mops his forehead with a napkin*) The universal formula.

EINSTEIN This is ludicrous. We've got hordes of highly paid physicists trying to make headway in gigantic state-supported laboratories, and you solve the whole thing en passant at your desk in this madhouse. (*He too mops his brow with a napkin.*)

NEWTON And the System of All Possible Inventions, Möbius?

MÖBIUS That exists too. I constructed it out of curiosity, as a practical companion piece to my theoretical works. Should I feign innocence? Thought has consequences. It was my duty to study the effects that my field theory and my theory of gravitation would produce. The result is devastating. New, inconceivable forces would be unleashed, enabling a technology that would dwarf all imagination, if my work were to fall into the hands of the human race.

EINSTEIN That can hardly be prevented.

NEWTON The only question is who gets hold of it first.

MÖBIUS (*laughing*) You would like your secret service to reap these benefits, wouldn't you, Kilton? And the general staff behind it?

NEWTON Why shouldn't I? Any general staff that finds a way to reintroduce the greatest physicist of all time to the scientific community is sacred to me.

EINSTEIN To me, only my own general staff is sacred. We provide the human race with enormous resources of power. That gives us the right to impose conditions. We must decide in whose favor we will apply our science, and I have made my decision.

NEWTON Nonsense, Eisler. The issue is freedom to pursue the cause of our science, that's all. Our job is to pioneer new developments, nothing else. Whether humanity knows how to follow the path we have prepared for it is humanity's business, not ours.

EINSTEIN You're a miserable aesthete, Kilton. If all you're concerned with is the freedom of science, why don't you join us? We, too, have stopped imposing party lines on our physicists, we can't afford to. We need results just as you do. Our political system eats from the hand of science, exactly like yours.

NEWTON Both our political systems, Eisler, must now eat out of Möbius's hand.

EINSTEIN On the contrary. He will have to obey us. We finally have him in check.

NEWTON Really? I think we have each other in check. Unfortunately, our secret services both came up with the same idea. If Möbius goes with you, I can do nothing about it, because you would stop me. And you would be helpless if Möbius decided in my favor. The choice is his, not ours.

EINSTEIN (*rising ceremoniously*)   Let's get the guns.

NEWTON (*also rising*)   Let's fight it out.

Newton retrieves the two revolvers from behind the fire screen and gives Einstein his weapon.

EINSTEIN I regret that this affair is coming to a bloody conclusion. But we must shoot. At each other, and certainly at our attendants. If necessary, even at Möbius. He may be the most important man in the world, but his manuscripts are more important.

MÖBIUS My manuscripts? I burned them.

Dead silence.

EINSTEIN Burned them?

MÖBIUS (*embarrassed*)   A little while ago. Before the police came back. As a precaution.

EINSTEIN (*bursts into despairing laughter*)   Burned.

NEWTON (*screaming with rage*)   Fifteen years of work.

EINSTEIN I'm going to lose my mind.

NEWTON Officially, we've already done that.

They put their guns in their pockets and sit down on the sofa, shattered.

EINSTEIN That means we're completely at your mercy, Möbius.

NEWTON   And for this I had to strangle a nurse and learn German.

EINSTEIN   While I had to learn to play the violin—which is torture for a person with no ear for music.

MÖBIUS   Shall we go on with dinner?

NEWTON   I've lost my appetite.

EINSTEIN   Too bad about the cordon bleu.

MÖBIUS (*stands up*)   We are three physicists. The decision we have to make is a decision among physicists. We must proceed scientifically. We must not allow ourselves to be swayed by opinions, but only by logical conclusions. We must try to find a rational solution. We cannot afford any errors in our thinking, because a wrong conclusion would lead to catastrophe. The fundamental premises are clear. All three of us have a single aim in view, but our tactics differ. That aim is the future of physics. You, Kilton, want to preserve the freedom of science, and argue that it has no responsibility. On the other hand you, Eisler, make physics answerable, in the name of responsibility, to the power politics of a particular country. Now what is the actual state of affairs? I need to know that if I am to make a decision.

NEWTON   Some of the most famous physicists are awaiting you. Remuneration and lodging are ideal. The climate is murderous, but the air-conditioning is excellent.

MÖBIUS   Are these physicists free?

NEWTON   My dear Möbius. These physicists have declared their willingness to solve scientific problems that are indispensable for our national defense. So you have to understand—

MÖBIUS So they're not free. (*He turns to Einstein.*)   Joseph Eisler. You are engaged in power politics. That requires power. Do you have power?

EINSTEIN You misunderstand me, Möbius. My power politics consists precisely in the fact that I have renounced my own power in favor of a party.

MÖBIUS Are you able to steer your party in accord with your sense of responsibility, or is there a danger of your being steered by your party?

EINSTEIN Möbius! That is ridiculous. Naturally I can only hope that the party will follow my recommendations, nothing more. Without hope it is impossible to hold any political position.

MÖBIUS Are your physicists free, at least?

EINSTEIN Well, to the extent that they, too, have to serve the national defense—

MÖBIUS Remarkable. Each of you is praising a different theory, but the actual conditions you have to offer are the same: a prison in either case. I prefer the madhouse. Here at least I can't be exploited by politicians.

EINSTEIN Certain risks do have to be taken.

MÖBIUS There are risks that must never be taken: the destruction of the human race is one of them. We know what the world is doing with the weapons it already has, and we can imagine what it would do with those that my research would make possible. This realization has determined all my actions. I was poor. I had a wife and three children. The university held out fame, industry beckoned with money. Both courses were too dangerous. I

63

would have had to publish my work, and the result would have been the overthrow of our system of knowledge and complete economic collapse. A sense of responsibility compelled me to take a different course. I dropped my academic career, turned my back on the industrial world, and abandoned my family to its fate. I put on the fool's cap. I pretended that King Solomon came to visit me, and was promptly locked up in a madhouse.

NEWTON   But that was no solution!

MÖBIUS   Reason demanded this step. In our science, we have run up against the limits of what is knowable. We know a few precisely definable laws, a few fundamental links between incomprehensible phenomena, that is all. The rest remains a mystery that baffles our understanding. We've come to the end of the road. But humanity hasn't caught up yet. We struggled onward and forward. But no one is following us; we have advanced into nothingness. Our science has become a horror, our research dangerous, our knowledge lethal. All that is left for us physicists is to capitulate before reality. Reality is no match for us. It comes to grief at our hands. We must take back our knowledge, and I have taken it back. There is no other solution, and that goes for you too.

EINSTEIN   What are you implying?

MÖBIUS   You have secret radio transmitters, am I right?

EINSTEIN   What of it?

MÖBIUS   Inform your superiors that you were mistaken, that I really am mad.

EINSTEIN   Then we'll be stuck here for the rest of our lives.

MÖBIUS   Quite probably.

EINSTEIN Nobody gives a damn about a failed spy.

MÖBIUS Exactly.

NEWTON So?

MÖBIUS You have to stay here in the madhouse with me.

NEWTON We?

MÖBIUS Both of you.

Silence.

NEWTON Möbius! You can't expect us to . . . for the rest of our—

MÖBIUS It's my only chance of remaining incognito. Only in the madhouse can we still be free. Only in the madhouse can we still afford to think. Outside, at liberty, our ideas are pure dynamite.

NEWTON But look, we're not crazy.

MÖBIUS But we *are* murderers.

They stare at him, taken aback.

NEWTON I resent that!

EINSTEIN You shouldn't have said that, Möbius!

MÖBIUS Anyone who kills is a murderer, and we have killed. Each of us came to this institution with a mission. Each of us killed his nurse for a definite purpose. You two did it so as not to endanger your secret mission, and I did it because Monika believed in me. She considered me an unrecognized genius. She didn't realize that today it is the duty of a genius to remain unrecognized. Killing is a horrible thing. I killed to prevent an even more horrible catastrophe. Now you've come along. I can't do away with you, but maybe I

65

can persuade you. Shall our murders become meaningless? Either we performed a sacrifice or it was murder. Either we remain in the madhouse or the world becomes a madhouse. Either we eliminate ourselves from the memory of mankind, or mankind eliminates itself.

Silence.

NEWTON Möbius!

MÖBIUS Yes, Kilton?

NEWTON This nuthouse. These horrible attendants. This hunchback doctor!

MÖBIUS Yes?

EINSTEIN We're caged in, like wild beasts!

MÖBIUS We *are* wild beasts. We should not be let loose on humanity.

Silence.

NEWTON Is there really no other solution?

MÖBIUS None.

Silence.

EINSTEIN Johann Wilhelm Möbius. I am a decent human being. I'm staying.

Silence.

NEWTON I'm staying too. For good.

Silence.

MÖBIUS Thank you. Thank you for giving the world a small chance of survival. (*He raises his glass.*)   To our nurses!

They have solemnly risen to their feet.

66

NEWTON I drink to Dorothea Moser.

THE TWO OTHERS To Dorothea!

NEWTON Dorothea! I had to sacrifice you. I requited your love with death! Now I want to prove myself worthy of you.

EINSTEIN I drink to Irene Straub.

THE TWO OTHERS To Irene!

EINSTEIN Irene! I had to sacrifice you. In your honor and in praise of your devotion, I will act rationally.

MÖBIUS I drink to Monika Stettler.

THE TWO OTHERS To Monika!

MÖBIUS Monika! I had to sacrifice you. May your love bless the friendship that we three physicists have formed in your name. Give us the strength to faithfully keep the secrets of our science in our guise as fools.

They drink and put the glasses on the table.

NEWTON Let us turn ourselves back into madmen. Let Newton haunt these rooms again.

EINSTEIN Let us fiddle away at Kreisler and Beethoven.

MÖBIUS Let Solomon's spirit appear to us again.

NEWTON Mad but wise.

EINSTEIN Imprisoned but free.

MÖBIUS Physicists but innocent.

The three men wave to each other and go to their rooms. The drawing room is empty. McArthur and Murillo enter right. They are now both wearing black uniforms, caps, and pistols. They clear off the table.

McArthur pushes the trolley with the china and cutlery off to the right. Murillo puts the round table in front of the window on the right, then places the upturned chairs on top of it, as if clearing up a restaurant after hours. Then Murillo, too, exits right. The room is empty again. Doctor Mathilde von Zahnd enters right, as always with white smock and stethoscope. She looks around. Finally Sievers comes in, also dressed in a black uniform.

UWE SIEVERS   Yes, boss.

DOCTOR VON ZAHND   The picture, Sievers.

McArthur and Murillo carry in a large portrait in a heavy gold frame. It represents a general. Sievers takes down the old portrait and puts up the new one.

DOCTOR VON ZAHND (*cont.*)   General Leonidas von Zahnd is better placed here than among the women. He still looks grand, the old warhorse, despite his goiter. He loved heroic deaths, and we've had three of those in this house. (*She gazes at her father's portrait.*)   The Privy Councillor, on the other hand, goes to the women's section among the millionairesses. Put him in the hallway for the time being.

McArthur and Murillo carry out the picture right.

DOCTOR VON ZAHND (*cont.*)   Has Director-General Fröben come with his heroes?

UWE SIEVERS   They are waiting in the green room. Shall I serve champagne and caviar?

DOCTOR VON ZAHND   The masterminds are here to work, not to feast.

She sits down on the sofa. McArthur and Murillo return from the right.

DOCTOR VON ZAHND (*cont.*)   Bring in the three patients, Sievers.

UWE SIEVERS   Yes, Ma'am! (*He goes to room number one, opens the door.*)   Möbius, come out!

McArthur and Murillo open doors two and three.

MURILLO   Newton, out!

MCARTHUR   Einstein, out!

Newton and Einstein come out. All three are in a state of exaltation.

NEWTON   A mysterious night. Infinite and sublime. Glittering through the bars of my window, Jupiter and Saturn reveal the laws of the universe.

EINSTEIN   A blissful night. Consoling and good. The riddles are silent, the questions are mute. I want to play my violin forever.

MÖBIUS   A solemn night. Deep blue and holy. The night of the mighty king. His white shadow detaches itself from the wall. His eyes are shining.

Silence.

DOCTOR VON ZAHND   Möbius. On the orders of the district attorney I may speak to you only in the presence of a guard.

MÖBIUS   I understand, Doctor von Zahnd.

DOCTOR VON ZAHND   But what I have to tell you also applies to your colleagues, Alec Jasper Kilton and Joseph Eisler.

They both stare at her in amazement.

NEWTON   You—know?

They both reach for their revolvers but are disarmed by Murillo and McArthur.

69

DOCTOR VON ZAHND   Gentlemen, your conversation was monitored. I was suspecting you for a long time. McArthur and Murillo, bring in Kilton's and Eisler's secret transmitters.

UWE SIEVERS   Hands behind your heads, the three of you!

Möbius, Einstein, and Newton put their hands behind their heads, McArthur and Murillo go into rooms two and three.

NEWTON   Droll! (*He laughs. Alone. An uncanny laugh.*)

EINSTEIN   I don't know—

NEWTON   Silly! (*Laughs again. Falls silent.*)

McArthur and Murillo return with the secret radio transmitters.

UWE SIEVERS   Hands down!

The physicists obey. Silence.

DOCTOR VON ZAHND   The searchlights, Sievers.

UWE SIEVERS   Okay, boss.

He raises his hand. Searchlights from outside bathe the physicists in blinding light. Simultaneously, Sievers switches off the lights inside.

DOCTOR VON ZAHND   The villa is surrounded by guards. Any attempt to escape is hopeless. (*to the male nurses*)   The three of you, out!

The three male nurses leave the room, carrying the weapons and instruments. Silence.

DOCTOR VON ZAHND   You alone shall learn my secret. Because it doesn't matter any longer whether you know it or not.

Silence.

DOCTOR VON ZAHND (*cont.*) (*solemnly*)   I, too, have received visitations from Solomon, the golden king.

All three stare at her in astonishment.

MÖBIUS   Solomon?

DOCTOR VON ZAHND   All these years.

Newton softly laughs.

DOCTOR VON ZAHND (*cont.*) (*undeterred*)   The first time was in my study. On a summer evening. Outside, the sun was still shining, and a woodpecker was hammering in the park, when suddenly the golden king came floating toward me. Like a tremendous angel.

EINSTEIN   She's lost her mind.

DOCTOR VON ZAHND   His gaze rested upon me. His lips opened. He began to speak to his handmaiden. He had risen from the dead, he intended to reclaim the power that was once his here below, he had revealed his wisdom so that Möbius would reign on earth in his name.

EINSTEIN   She has to be locked up. She belongs in an asylum.

DOCTOR VON ZAHND   But Möbius betrayed him. He tried to conceal what could not be concealed. For what was revealed to him is no secret. Because it is thinkable. What is thinkable will some day be thought. Now or in the future. What Solomon had discovered could be discovered by someone else. But it was to remain the deed of the golden king, the means toward the establishment of his holy dominion, and so he sought me out, his unworthy handmaiden.

EINSTEIN (*urgently*)   You are mad. Do you hear me? You are mad.

DOCTOR VON ZAHND The golden king commanded me to depose Möbius and rule in his place. I obeyed. I was a doctor and Möbius was my patient. I could do with him as I wished. I sedated him for years, again and again, and made photocopies of the golden king's writings, down to the last page.

NEWTON You're out of your mind! Completely! Don't you understand?! (*softly*) We're *all* out of our minds.

DOCTOR VON ZAHND I went about it cautiously. At first I exploited only two or three discoveries, to bring in the necessary capital. Then I founded huge industrial plants, bought one factory after another, and established a powerful cartel. Gentlemen, I will make full use of the System of All Possible Inventions.

MÖBIUS (*urgently*) Doctor Mathilde von Zahnd: You are sick. Solomon does not exist. He never appeared to me.

DOCTOR VON ZAHND You are lying.

MÖBIUS I just invented him in order to keep my discoveries secret.

DOCTOR VON ZAHND You are denying him.

MÖBIUS Listen to reason. Acknowledge that you are insane.

DOCTOR VON ZAHND No more than you are.

MÖBIUS Then I will have to shout the truth to the world. You have exploited me all these years. Shamelessly. You even let my poor wife pay for me.

DOCTOR VON ZAHND You are powerless, Möbius. Even if your voice were to penetrate these walls, the world would not believe you. Because to the public at large you are nothing but a dangerous lunatic. Because of the murder you committed.

The truth dawns on the three men.

MÖBIUS   Monika?

EINSTEIN   Irene?

NEWTON   Dorothea?

DOCTOR VON ZAHND   I simply made use of an opportunity. The wisdom of Solomon had to be safeguarded and your treachery punished. I had to render the three of you harmless. Through your murders. I incited those three nurses against you. I could count on you to act as you did. You were as predictable as robots and you killed like professional hit men.

Einstein restrains Möbius, who was about to assault the doctor.

DOCTOR VON ZAHND (*cont.*)   There is no point in attacking me, Möbius. Just as there was no point in burning manuscripts I had already copied.

Möbius turns away.

DOCTOR VON ZAHND (*cont.*)   What you see around you are no longer the walls of a mental institution. This house is the treasury of my cartel. It encloses three physicists, the only human beings apart from myself who know the truth. What holds you in check are not psychiatric attendants: Sievers is the head of my industrial police. You have fled into a prison of your own making. Solomon thought through you, acted through you, and now he is destroying you. Through me.

Silence. In a tone of serene piety, Doctor von Zahnd continues.

DOCTOR VON ZAHND (*cont.*) But I am assuming his power. I am not afraid. My institution is full of mad relatives, all of them bedecked with jewels and medals. I am the last normal person in my family. The end product. Barren, suitable only for the love of my neighbor. But Solomon took pity on me. He who has a thousand wives chose me. Now I will be more powerful than my forefathers. My cartel will rule, will conquer nations and continents, exploit the solar system, send spaceships to Andromeda. The experiment has been a success, not for the world, but for a hunchbacked old maid. (*She rings a little bell.*)

Uwe Sievers enters right.

UWE SIEVERS Yes, boss?

DOCTOR VON ZAHND Let's go, Sievers. The board of directors is waiting. My global enterprise is under way, the wheels of production are rolling. (*She exits right with Uwe Sievers.*)

The three physicists are alone. Silence. There are no options left.

NEWTON It's over. (*He sits down on the sofa.*)

EINSTEIN The world has fallen into the hands of an insane psychiatrist. (*He sits down next to Newton.*)

MÖBIUS Whatever has once been thought can never be taken back. (*He sits down in the armchair on the left of the sofa.*)

Silence. They stare into space. Then they speak, quite calmly and naturally, simply introducing themselves to the audience.

NEWTON I am Newton. Sir Isaac Newton. Born January fourth, sixteen forty-three, at Woolsthorpe, near Grantham. I am president of the Royal Society. But there's no need to rise on my account. I wrote *The Mathematical Principles of Natural Philosophy*. I said: "Hypotheses non fingo." In the fields of experimental optics, theoretical mechanics, and higher mathematics my achievements are not insignificant. But the question of the nature of gravity I had to leave unresolved. I also wrote theological books. Commentaries on the prophet Daniel and on the Revelation of Saint John the Divine. I am Newton. Sir Isaac Newton. I am president of the Royal Society. (*He rises and goes into his room.*)

EINSTEIN   I am Einstein. Professor Albert Einstein. Born March fourteenth, eighteen seventy-nine in Ulm. In nineteen hundred and two I secured a position as an examiner in the Federal Patent Office in Bern. There I worked out my special theory of relativity, which transformed the nature of physics. Then I became a member of the Prussian Academy of Sciences. Later I became a refugee. Because I am a Jew. It was I who developed the formula $E = mc^2$, the key to the transformation of matter into energy. I love humanity and I love my violin, but it was on my recommendation that the atom bomb was built. I am Einstein. Professor Albert Einstein. Born March fourteenth, eighteen seventy-nine in Ulm. (*He rises and goes into his room. Then he is heard playing his violin. Kreisler. Liebeslied.*)

MÖBIUS   I am Solomon. I am poor King Solomon. I was once immeasurably rich, wise, and God-fearing. My power caused the mighty to tremble. I was a prince of peace and justice. But my wisdom destroyed my fear of God, and when I no longer feared God, my wisdom destroyed my wealth. Now the cities I ruled are dead, the kingdom entrusted to me has become an empty, blue-shimmering desert, and somewhere around a small, yellow, nameless star there circles, pointlessly, constantly, the radioactive earth. I am Solomon, I am Solomon, I am poor King Solomon. (*He goes into his room.*)

Now the drawing room is empty. All that can be heard is Einstein's violin.

The End